AF365408
LAND
of the
GNOMES

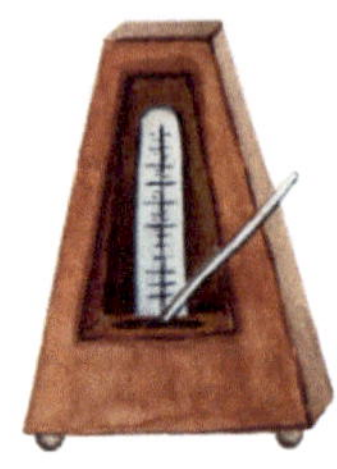

"Thank you, Fontaine Wallace, my
wonderful mother and editor." – M.W.C.

Find Children's Books, Novels, and Short Stories at Amazon, Barnes & Noble, Walmart, Simon & Schuster, Target, and at: www.MicheleCampanelli.com

www.SlothDreamsBooks.com

Copyright © 2024 by Michele Wallace Campanelli
Illustrations by KeriAnne N. Jelinek
Cover Design by KeriAnne N. Jelinek

Published by Sloth Dreams Books & Publishing, LLC.
Sloth Dreams Children's Books
Pennsylvania, USA
www.SlothDreamsBooks.com

ISBN: 978-7-1671-2514-2

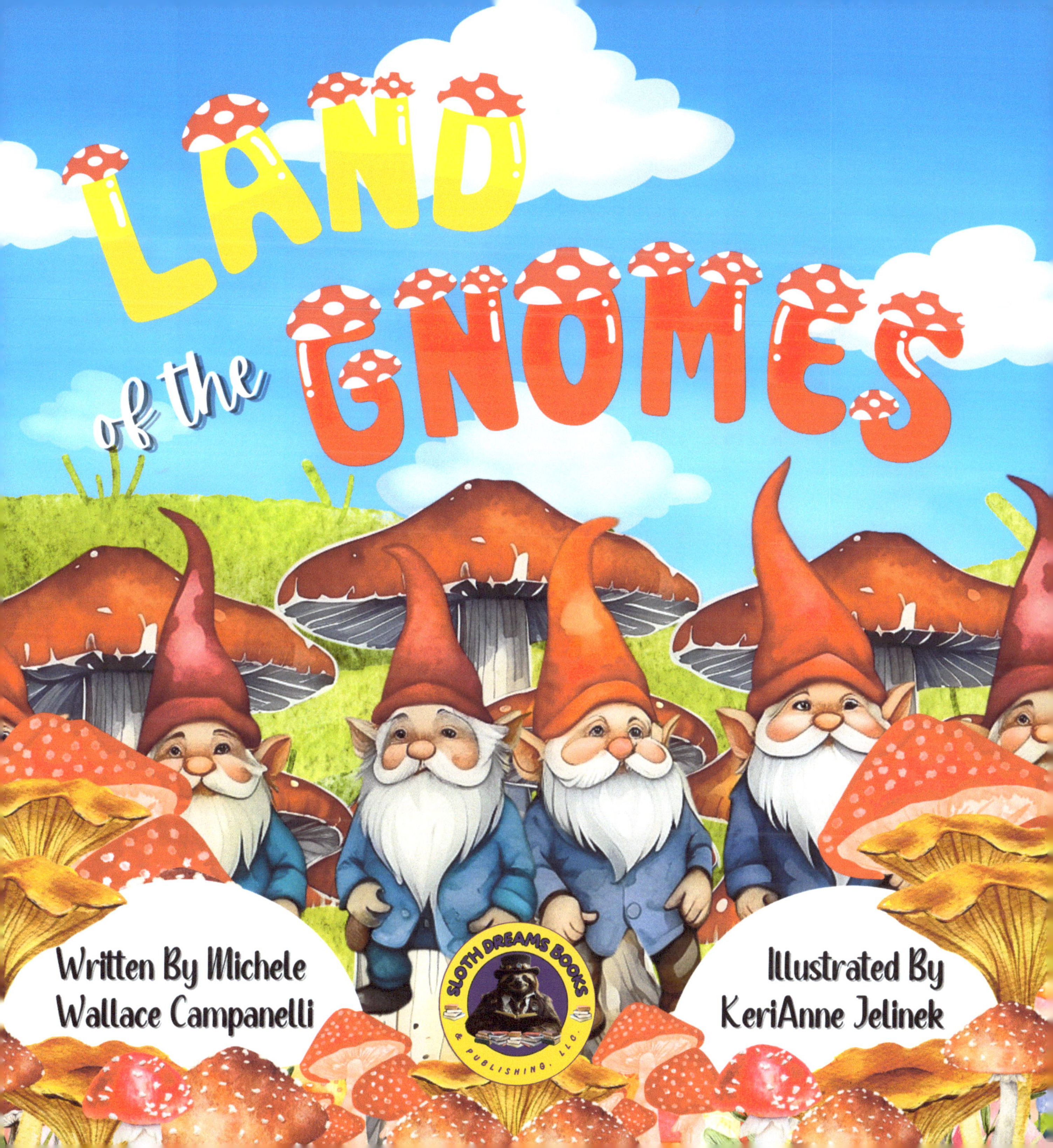

LAND
of the
GNOMES
Written By Michele Wallace Campanelli
SLOTH DREAMS BOOKS & PUBLISHING, LLC.
Illustrated By KeriAnne Jelinek

Once upon a time, in the land next to Mr. Maelzel's quaint home, a small group of gnomes lived.

Gnomes are small human-like beings who wear colorful clothing and big red shoes. They live in mushroom houses in a garden.

Once they reach the age of two, they become completely white-haired. Their tummies get quite round, and they love spending time amongst the colorful flowers.

A friendly and happy bunch, gnomes live in harmony with one another in small groups, usually near a source of water for watering big mushrooms and plants.

Gnomes have only one fear... that humans might discover their village and ask them to leave... or worse, tell someone that they exist.

One day in May, underneath a large mushroom
on Mr. Maelzel's property, a tiny golden
trumpet sounded; it was being played by a young
gnome who announced the birth of a new baby.

Excitedly, all dozen gnomes gathered outside the mushroom home of Suzette and Cartra gnome to get a glimpse of the new infant.

This was a gnome custom to greet the new baby in the village, but today, something different occurred. The door was locked. Outside the mushroom house the screech owl sat.

"Is something wrong with Suzette?" Cartra gnome asked the owl doorkeeper.

"With the baby," the owl replied.

"Something's wrong with his gnome belly!"

"Is it not plump like the rest of us?" a gnome asked.

"Come now, let us see the new member of our gnome family."

"Isn't he fit to work in the garden?" another gnome asked.

"I'm not sure," the owl replied. "I was told to tell everyone to go away."

"Nonsense!" One gnome stepped up to pound on the door of the home of Suzette and Cartra.

Suddenly, the door in the stem of a mushroom opened and out came Cartra with a baby gnome wrapped in flower petals.

"This is my new son," Cartra exclaimed proudly. All the gnomes cheered.

"He's a fine gnome," announced one.

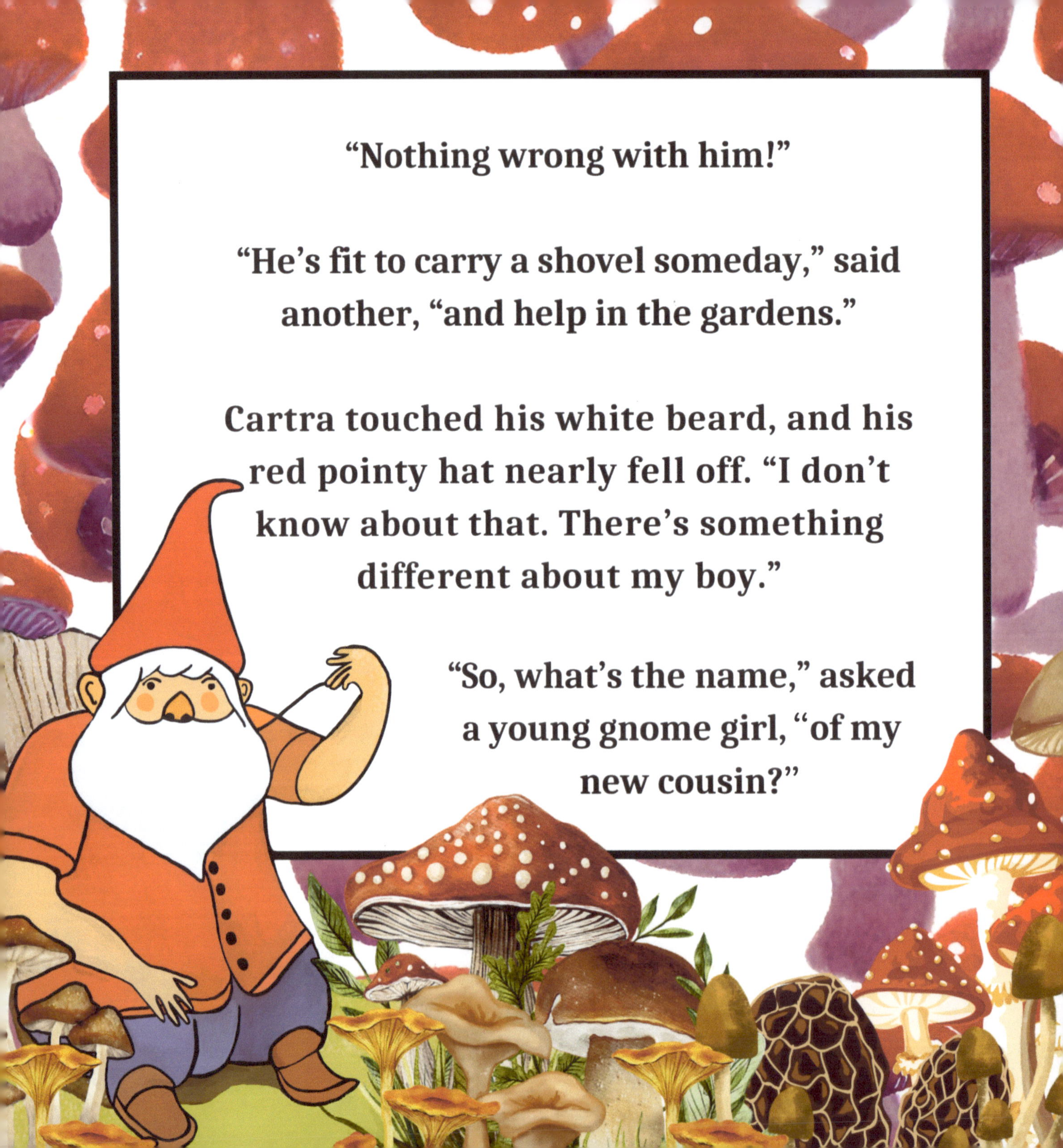

"Nothing wrong with him!"

"He's fit to carry a shovel someday," said another, "and help in the gardens."

Cartra touched his white beard, and his red pointy hat nearly fell off. "I don't know about that. There's something different about my boy."

"So, what's the name," asked a young gnome girl, "of my new cousin?"

"We've named him Metra," announced Cartra the new father.

"We heard something was wrong with his belly? Can we see?" asked the gnome cook.

"How's Suzette?"

"Suzette is well. That will come another day," Cartra the gnome announced.

"Thank you all for coming, but my family needs rest."

For days, the gnomes went
about their business.

They planted flower seeds,
played with bugs, and made
sure the bees found the
best pollen to make honey.

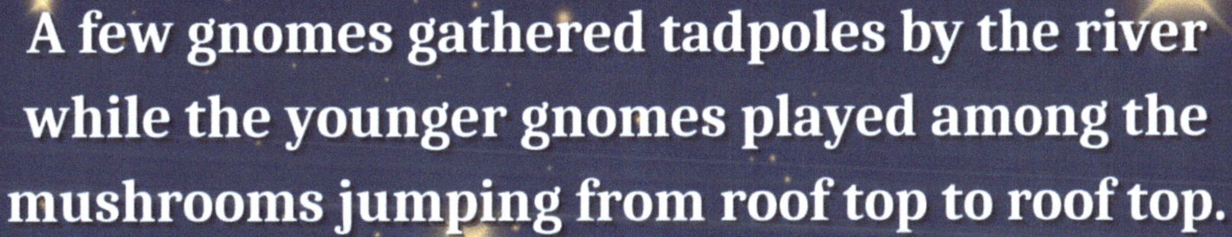

A few gnomes gathered tadpoles by the river while the younger gnomes played among the mushrooms jumping from roof top to roof top.

The usual cheerful lives of the garden gnomes continued, yet there was something slightly different in the air, especially at dark night.

When the moon shone in the sky, a never-heard-before noise sounded. All the gnomes knew that this strange noise was coming from inside the Cartra gnome family mushroom since the baby had been born. Was it a click?

Click! Click!

"What do you think is happening in there?" a gnome questioned the screech owl who sat in the tree above.

"I do not know," hooted the owl. "It's happened only since the birth of the baby."

"You are the wise one. You must know."

"Look! Mr. Maelzel comes now from his house to the creek. Hurry hide!" warned the owl.

"He must have heard the noise, too!"

Click! Click!

As footsteps tapped down the hill, the gnomes hid underneath the biggest mushrooms. One shoe was only a foot away, so the nearest gnome covered his mouth to try to stop himself from making a peep.

Click! Click!

Suddenly, a tick sounded from inside the Cartra mushroom home. "Oh, no!" A worried expression crossed the face of the gnome.

"There's that noise! Where is that coming from?"

It didn't take long for Mr. Maelzel to lean down and pick up the mushroom, the house of Cartra and Suzette Gnome.

Suddenly, Cartra and Suzette jumped out and rushed to hide underneath a nearby mushroom, but the little baby was still inside in his crib.

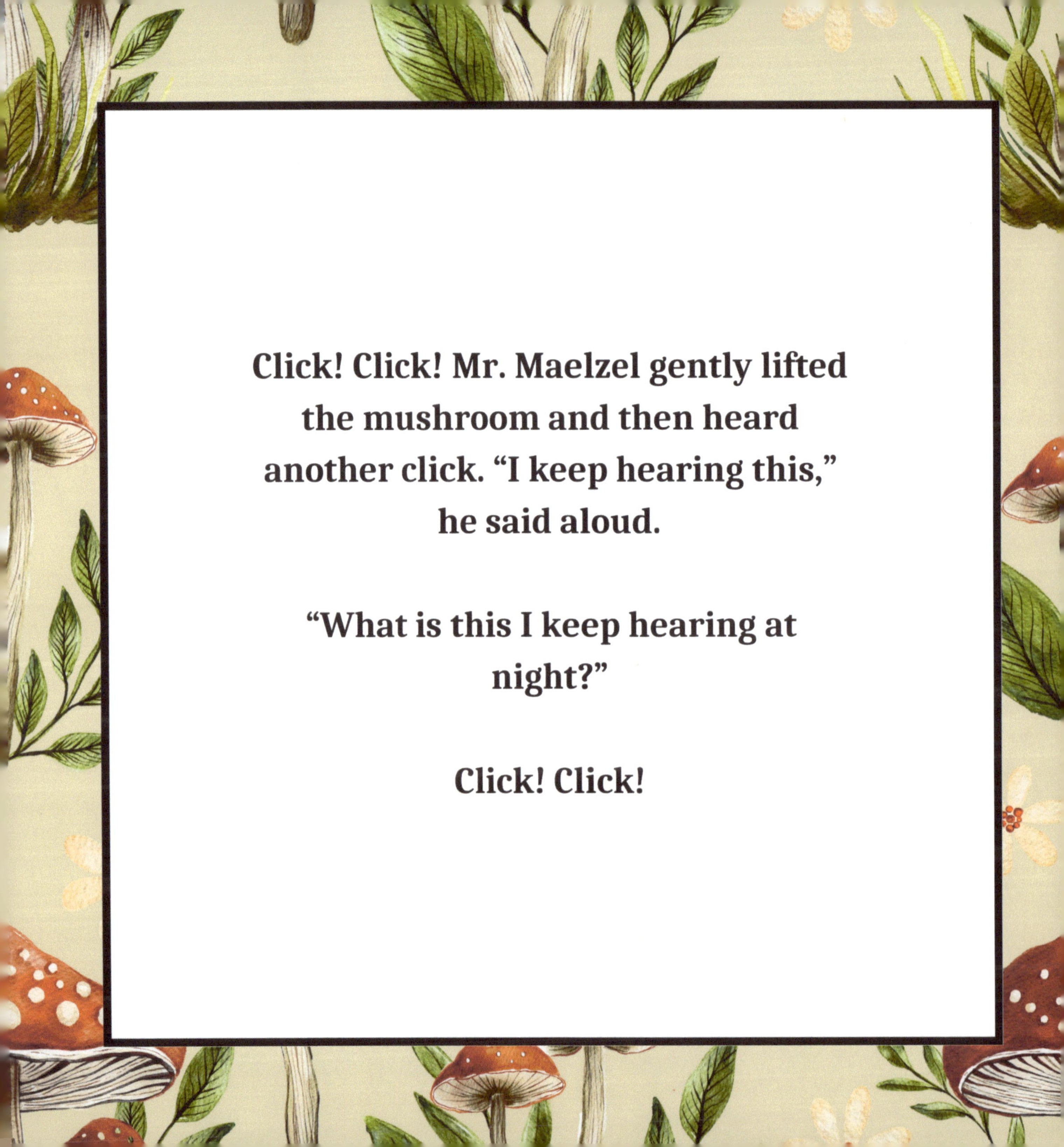

Click! Click! Mr. Maelzel gently lifted the mushroom and then heard another click. "I keep hearing this," he said aloud.

"What is this I keep hearing at night?"

Click! Click!

Discovering more noises, Mr. Maelzel ripped
off the mushroom roof to see what was causing
the unusual sounds.

"What a magical thing!" gasped Mr. Maelzel
when he saw Metra in his crib covered in flower
petals. He carefully lifted the baby in his palm.

"A strange baby gnome! I thought you
lived only in fairy tales!"

Suddenly the click sounded again, and this time, the human pushed away the flower petals from off the top of the baby. His belly revealed what looked to be a stick which swung from side to side. Now with the petals gone, Mr. Maelzel could see that it was the baby making those strange noises in perfect timing!

Click. Click.

Then again, the stick went from right to left.

Click. Click!

And then repeated, over and over until Mr. Maelzel pushed the stick back into place. "Oh, what rhythm you have! Perfect rhythm!" Mr. Maelzel said.

"What a talented gnome child! You must come home with me."

It was a great surprise to all the gnomes when Mr. Maelzel gently carried the baby gnome up the hill and into his house, out of view of his parents.

"What will he do to our son?" asked Suzette to her husband.

"Humans don't eat gnomes, so I'm sure he'll be fine."

"I want to make sure my son is safe," Suzette cried. "We must get him back!"

"Let's all make sure he's okay," replied the owl. "We'll take the baby back by force if necessary."

In one long line, a dozen gnomes and the owl
walked up the hill and crawled up to sit on
the windowsill of Mr. Maelzel's home.

The human was behind the piano with his fingers playing a simple tune. Metra was on the top of the piano, his tummy ticking like a time machine, clicking left and right. Surprisingly, the baby wasn't scared at all. He was happily smiling and clapping along with his tummy. The baby even started laughing; his parents had never seen him so happy!

"Metra is keeping the beat of the music," Cartra announced. "He even likes it! Look at that! My son does have talent, just like Mr. Maelzel said."

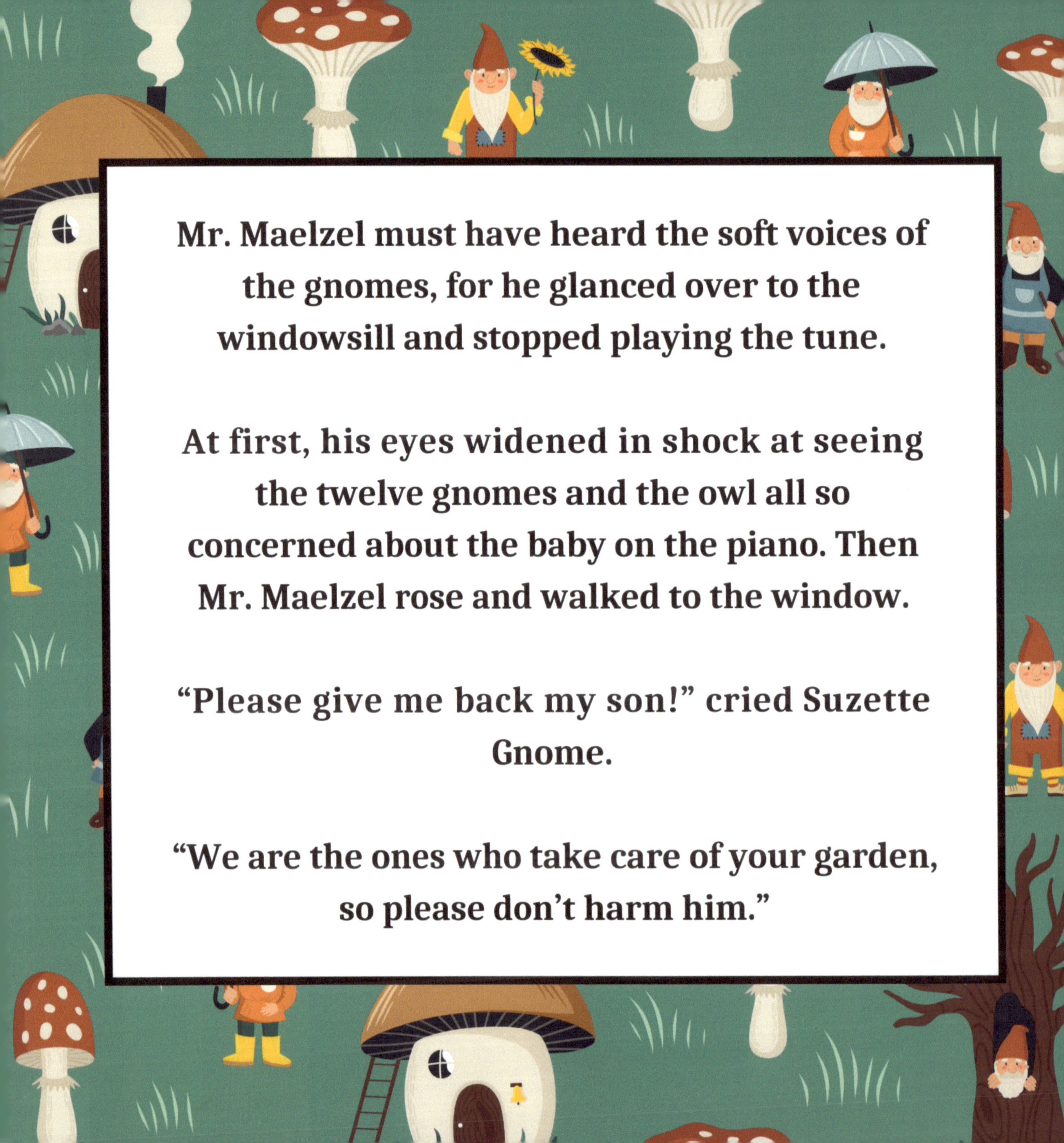

Mr. Maelzel must have heard the soft voices of the gnomes, for he glanced over to the windowsill and stopped playing the tune.

At first, his eyes widened in shock at seeing the twelve gnomes and the owl all so concerned about the baby on the piano. Then Mr. Maelzel rose and walked to the window.

"Please give me back my son!" cried Suzette Gnome.

"We are the ones who take care of your garden, so please don't harm him."

Mr. Maelzel picked up the baby gnome gently in his hand and gave him back to Suzette.

"He's a very talented little gnome, very musically inclined. Bring him back to me every night so he can keep my time while I practice."

The baby gnome raised his arms toward Mr. Maelzel, a sure sign he liked him enough to want to be returned.

"All right, he does seem to like you and your playing," Suzette said. "I will let my son be your musical guest as long as you let us gnomes live in peace by the creek. You must never harm another one of our mushroom homes ever again or mention us to anyone."

"Agreed," said Mr. Maelzel with a happy smile. "I just want to practice piano with the baby and make drawings so that I can show his amazing belly. What is this gnome baby's name by the way?"

"His name is Metra," Cartra the gnome announced.

"Metra-gnome will be the name of my invention then, after your talented son."

So, in the land of gnomes, on the property of Mr. Maelzel, the Metra-Gnome was discovered. Mr. Maelzel created a rhythm machine inspired by a gnome's belly which came to be used by all musicians around the world. The "Metronome" would help keep better time for centuries to come.

Johann N. Maelzel, a German engineer and prolific entertainer, invented and manufactured the metronome and other interesting musical machines which he became famous for.

In 1813 Maelzel also co-wrote "The Battle of Vitoria" with Ludwig Van Beethoven.

Together, Beethoven and Maelzel performed numerous concerts in which Beethoven's symphonies included Maelzel's unique automaton musical inventions.

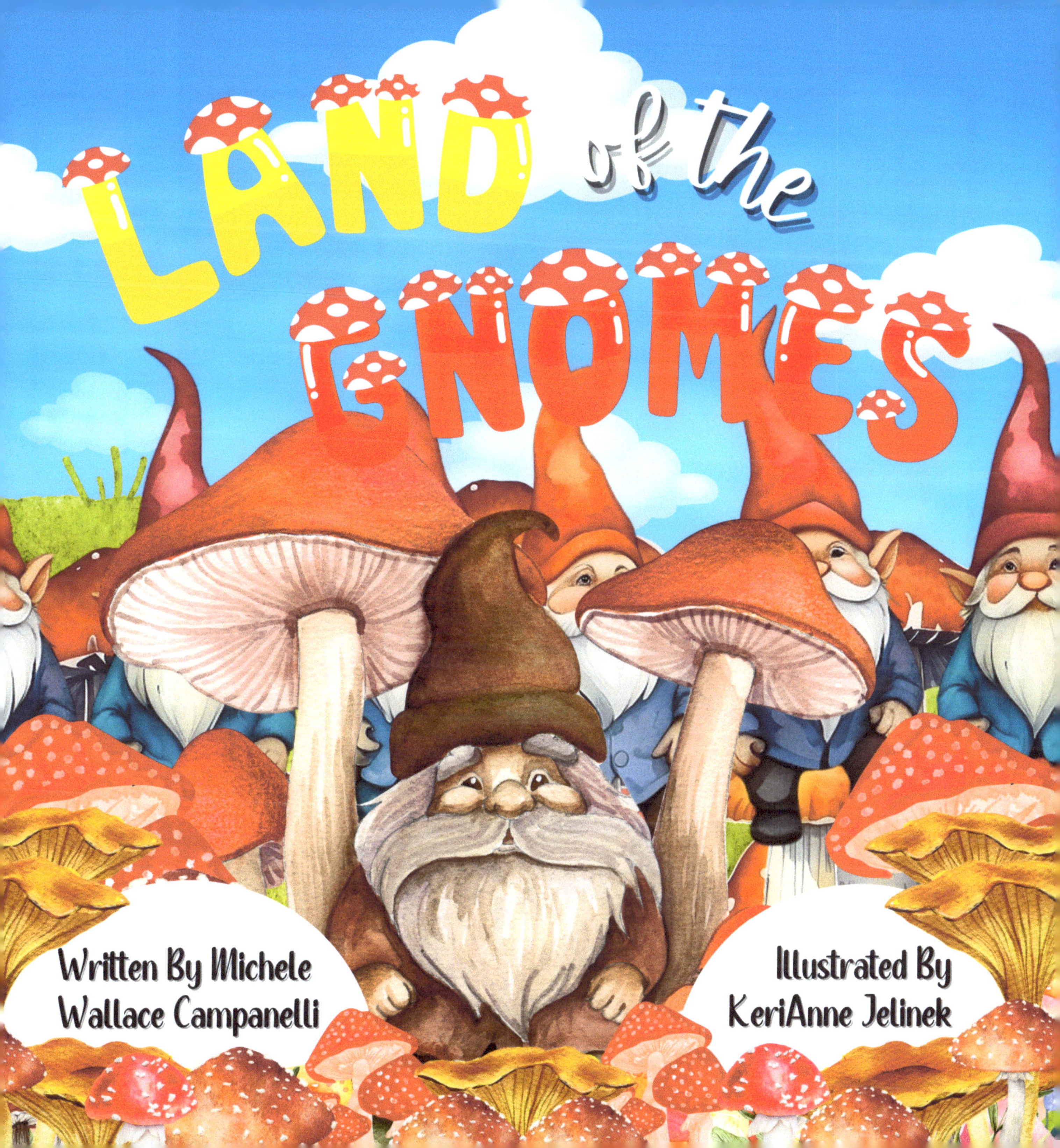

LAND of the GNOMES
Written By Michele Wallace Campanelli
Illustrated By KeriAnne Jelinek

Metronomes
I'm an Old-Fashioned Metronome
I'm an Electronic or Digital Metronome
I'm a Modern Metronome

About the Author

Michele Wallace Campanelli is an American writer, singer, and celebrity. During the early 1990s, she started writing short stories and fiction novels professionally. She has had nine stories appearing on the best-sellers list, including two that reached #1 on the New York Times. Her short stories have been included in over 30 international selling anthologies. She has also penned numerous novels, magazine and newspaper articles in both fiction and non-fiction published by Simon & Schuster, Chronicle Books, Fireside Books, Fictionwise, Whiskey Creek Press, Wee Creek Press, Florida Today Newspaper, Woman's World Magazine, Adamsmedia, McGraw-Hill, Multnomah Books, Red Rock Press, HCI and America House Publishing. Over 57 million people have read her written works internationally. When Michele isn't writing, she is CEO of Regal Entertainment Services LLC. and Social Media Director of the Space Coast Symphony Orchestra. Michele's books can be found at:
www.MicheleCampanelli.com

Michele Wallace Campanelli
Author

About the Illustrator

KeriAnne N. Jelinek is a highly accomplished figure in the world of children's literature, distinguished as a best-selling author and illustrator, an astute publisher, and sought-after book consultant. As the CEO/Founder of Sloth Dreams Books & Publishing, LLC, she has steered the creation and self-publication of an impressive catalogue of over 160 children's books since January 2022, marking a significant imprint on the literary landscape. Her dedication to the craft extends beyond writing, encompassing roles as an illustrator, editor, and cover designer, showcasing her comprehensive understanding of the publishing industry. She has been seen on news stations, podcasts, radio channels throughout the USA, and the UK. Her books are in libraries, bookstores, and sold around the world. Her books can be found on Amazon, Barnes & Noble, Books-A-Million, Baker and Taylor, Walmart, Target, and so much more. She maintains an active podcast for children entitled "Sloths Love to Read", a YouTube channel, an educational blog, and promotes other self-published authors via book consulting, coaching, publishing, courses, and more! KeriAnne's books can be found at: www.SlothDreamsBooks.com

KeriAnne N. Jelinek
Illustrator